LIVING
IN A
COMPLEX
WORLD

Joachim Winkler

LIVING IN A COMPLEX WORLD

A SIMPLE GUIDE

Pen, Plot and Pixel

First published in the UK in 2015 by Pen, Plot and Pixel,
181 St Albans Avenue, Chiswick, London W4 5JT

ISBN paperback 978 1 909105 03 4
ISBN ebook 978 1 909105 04 1

You can find out more about the author and publisher at
the following website www.penplotandpixel.com

A CIP catalogue record for this title is available from the British Library

Printed and bound by CPI Group (UK) Ltd, Croydon CR0 4YY

Preface

For thousands of years people in towns and in the countryside lived in small communities, within which they had their work, family and friends. Their lives were based on the understanding that they were in this world to survive by working, praying and on Sundays, resting. Life was disciplined by the simple fact of not being able to spend more than one earned. People lived by values and laws established by religions and rulers, such as the Ten Commandments, or human values such as honesty, reliability, loyalty, respect. Life may have been hard, but the underlying structural guidelines to how one should live one's life were simple. Today, these are still the guidelines for thousands of communities.

However in the twentieth century, after two world wars, the western world changed drastically. Under serious economic pressure governments wanted to be free to act as they saw fit, and not to be restricted by financial rules. The gold standard was done away with, thereby removing the need for financial discipline from governments and banks.

Social-minded governments improved life for many people by regulating working and living conditions, however governments were also pushing for growth in consumer markets, creating and feeding the desire from the majority for more and more possessions. This century has seen the huge expansion in digital developments that has led to massive growth in the entertainment and communication industries, and the spread of knowledge and information to, and from, all corners of the globe. People who live in small communities are now subjected to pressures from all around the world that affect their expectations and desires.

These changes in the way people live have led individuals, organisations and governments to amass huge debts. In turn, these lead to exposure, vulnerability and uncertainty, something no government and no individual seems able to deal with. In addition, lack of time and the good management of time have now become the over-riding problem. These changes have created today's complex world, with its pressures and anxieties and often, unhappiness and discontent.

However I firmly believe that the traditional values and guidelines, which underpinned our communities for hundreds of years, are still valid, and now more necessary than ever in helping people cope with today's challenges.

In 1990, when I saw that these economic and social developments had eliminated or changed the meaning of traditional values, rules and behaviour and, moreover, that many schools did not provide education on these subjects any longer, I started discussions with my own children on some of these subjects based on what I had learned from my parents, my years in school and my life experience. This book is a simple record of these discussions. My guidelines are personal and I do not claim they are right for everyone. In fact, every person should be encouraged to work out their own guidelines and go their own way — the important thing is to think about one's own path through life and how best to follow it.

This book is not meant to entertain, but to encourage people to think about each particular subject under discussion. Therefore it may be advisable to read just one or two chapters at a time.

Joachim Winkler

Contents

The Boat
(with thanks to Khalil Gibran)

A boat is driven by the wind in its sails and steered by a rudder. In life, the sail can be compared to feelings, passions and enthusiasm, while the rudder, which determines the boat's direction, can be compared to reason.

If a boat had only a sail, it would be propelled forward by the wind and would move. However, without a rudder, it would be impossible to determine the direction, and the boat could only move in a random way, quite likely round in circles.

If a boat only had a rudder and no sails, it could determine its direction, but it would be unable to move towards its destination.

Life is similar.

Your sail, which is your feelings, your passions and your enthusiasm, will cause you to be active and to move, but you will not know where you are headed.

Likewise, with just a rudder or your reason on its own, you will not move forward through life.

To succeed in life you need both. The sail to move

you forwards and the rudder to steer you towards your destination.

Sometimes you need more sails (more drive or passion), to reach your destination, and sometimes you will have to use the rudder to change direction (apply reason to a situation), in order to remain on track towards your destination.

Sometimes these forces may contradict one another — passion may want you to go in one direction, while reason tells you to go a different way. Your entire life will therefore be affected by your ability to synchronise your passion and your reason, to create a balance that moves you forwards in the right direction.

With some people, their passage through life will be full of vigorous swings, from passion to reason and back again. Others will experience more moderate swings between these two forces. If you can achieve a balance, you should be able to move forwards towards your goal in life.

Wealth and Poverty

It is important to consider not only physical and material wealth and poverty, but also spiritual and emotional wealth and poverty.

From a purely physical, materialistic point of view, living a good life means having enough food to nourish your body, a roof over your head, and sufficient clothing to keep you warm. If you are rich, you also have luxuries — perhaps your own home, a car, a computer, a television, nice clothes, regular holidays, and on top of that savings, which can relieve you of many worries.

If you are poor, you do not have all these things. You may not have enough money for basics such as food and clothing. The poorest of the poor do not even have a roof over their head.

Food, shelter and clothing are our three basic physical needs and without them, life will be a struggle.

From a spiritual and emotional point of view, if you are healthy, happy and satisfied with your life and your environment (whatever your level of material wealth), you are rich.

If you are unhealthy, unhappy and dissatisfied with your life (whatever your level of material wealth), you are spiritually and emotionally poor.

Material wealth does not automatically give you spiritual and emotional wealth. On the contrary, it may remove your impetus and motivation to finding a healthier, happier, more satisfying life, leading to a high degree of dissatisfaction.

Greed and fear are among the most serious threats to living a satisfying emotional life — one comes from internal forces, one from external.

Greed makes you chase after more and more material wealth, never satisfied with what you already have. It prevents you enjoying your life and enjoying what you do have, and stops you finding peace of mind.

Fear is even worse. It constricts you mentally and can paralyse you to such an extent that you cannot move freely through your life. It can remove your ability to find enjoyment and satisfaction in anything. The ability to live without fear is an essential and basic right for everyone.

The most important goal in life is to find spiritual and emotional satisfaction — this in turn will bring you happiness and peace of mind.

Controlling your Thoughts

You alone control your thoughts.

You alone can change your way of thinking.

If you have unpleasant thoughts, you can change them immediately by shifting them to something pleasant, such as a happy event, a favourite television programme, or a much-loved story — something you know you enjoy.

This ability to direct your thoughts can be used to reduce the size of problems or even get rid of them altogether. You may only be facing a small problem, but the more you think about it, the larger it becomes — you could be making a mountain out of a molehill. If you stop thinking about the problem, it retreats into the background and shrinks.

Many problems are solved by time. Therefore, it is advisable to practise patience when dealing with problems.

Learn a lesson from the bear. If a bear touches a hot stone, he will press it against his chest, but this only makes matters worse.

If you are faced with a problem, do not clutch it to your

chest and turn your thoughts to it continuously. This will only make the problem appear larger and more significant. Learn to do the opposite, by dropping the hot stone, or problem.

Push the problem out of your mind and replace it with happier thoughts. It is quite possible that, as time goes by, the problem will solve itself, or a solution will come to you unbidden.

When I was young and had to make an important decision, I was advised to sleep on it. After that I always tried to allow at least 24 hours to pass before making a major decision and this helped me to make the right choices.

Relax

Now we come to one of the most important behavioural rules in life.

You will know that if you want to achieve something that involves physical effort, you have to use physical energy.

However the opposite rule applies to mental and spiritual activities; you have to relax in order to get results. Tension can have a negative impact on your brain's reasoning power. If you are not in a relaxed state of mind, your brain becomes less efficient and your thinking abilities are greatly reduced.

To illustrate this, think of sporting events where high performance is required all the time, for example motor racing. The best drivers are those who can relax — they drive around the track with a controlled calmness, even at extremely high speeds.

When you were completing an exam paper, you might write down everything you could think of, but could find you were still struggling with some questions. However if you relaxed, you would often find the answers would then come to mind.

The reason for this is that your mind has both conscious and subconscious thought processes. The subconscious mind stores everything you have ever seen, read or experienced and so is a treasure trove of knowledge.

On the other hand, your conscious mind remembers things you have heard or experienced repeatedly, and those matters that are of special importance to you.

In an exam you would be using your conscious mind, thinking hard, making deductions and trying to answer the questions. But if you could relax and tap into your subconscious mind, which stores so much more information, you would be able to access this deeper knowledge and use it to find answers.

Any type of tension constricts you, restraining not only the muscles of the body, but also of the mind. If you are able to relax, take a deep breath and turn to other thoughts for a few moments, it can help to clear your conscious mind, opening up your subconscious and leading to a more productive way of thinking.

The Guide Beam

A plane finds its way from one airport to another by following a guide beam. As it is often impossible for the pilot to see the earth below, the plane has to follow the beam, which is transmitted to the plane from the ground stations. If the plane deviates from the beam it may run into great danger, as it then cannot find the way to its destination.

Our lives also follow a direction, or guide beam. However our guide beam is determined by ourselves and can change from time to time. If we change our guide beam, we can change the direction of our life.

Regardless of the direction, our guide beam should always be attached to certain values that we allow to lead us through our lives. These include values such as:
- trust
- honesty
- reliability
- flexibility
- modesty

- punctuality
- cleanliness

There are many other values that might matter to you. The values that guide each of us are those that are important to us personally. They serve as our guide beam, telling us whether our lives are on the right track. When we deviate from these values, our guide beam should activate our instincts and common sense, making us aware we are not on the right track.

However, the beam is not just a thin line. On the contrary, it is as wide as a carriageway. Although it is preferable to move along the middle of this road, we actually move from left to right and right to left, as we are often unable to control our actions with precision. If we move too far to the right side of our carriageway, we have to correct it by steering a little towards the left. Should we move too far to the left, we need to steer over to the right. We are always trying to return to the central line, travelling along our guide beam like a car travelling along the central line of a carriageway.

Should we move off our guide beam completely and 'come off the road', perhaps because we lost sight of our values or took a wrong turn in life, it can be quite difficult to find the way back. In order to return to the right path, we may have to retrace our steps to find out where we went wrong and see why and where we got lost. We can then pick up our guide beam again.

Everyone can understand that the shortest distance between two points is a straight line. The more we deviate from a straight line, the longer our path will be. There are people who move in circles, and never reach their destination, because they constantly get lost or go over the same ground again and again. In all likelihood they have no clear destination in mind, making it virtually impossible for them to find a guide beam to follow.

If you have a clear destination in mind, and stick to the values that direct your life, you should find it easy to follow your own guide beam.

The Seven Laws
(with thanks to Emmet Fox)

In these Seven Laws you will find references to the guidelines I have already outlined. These Seven Laws determine not only our values, but also our way of thinking.

1. The Law of Substitution

It is not always easy simply to abandon a certain thought. It is much easier to replace one thought with another, more positive one. If your mind turns to negative thoughts, such as, 'I don't want to go to work today,' you could replace this thought with another, such as, 'I am looking forward to this evening's football game.'

By doing this, you have replaced a negative thought with a positive one. As soon as you realise that your mind is wandering to something unpleasant or negative, you don't want it to grow more dominant by constantly brooding on it, so replace that thought with something pleasant, cheerful and positive.

2. The Law of Relaxation

When you apply mental pressure, the accompanying tension can prevent your mind from working to its full capacity. If you realise that stress and tension are taking over, one way to relax is to turn your mind to cheerful and happy thoughts. Think about a place or person you love, or an activity you like, or a sport you enjoy playing.

3. The Law of Subconscious Activity

While we are awake we have an ever-present conscious mind that determines our decisions. In addition, we possess a considerably more valuable asset, in the form of a subconscious mind, which stores all our experiences and data.

This subconscious mind has the ability to work with all your accumulated knowledge and can even come to conclusions unbidden. While you are asleep, your conscious mind is asleep too. However at this time, without your awareness, your subconscious mind is active and constantly tries to solve problems and tasks that confront it. As soon as an idea starts forming in your head, your subconscious immediately starts work, using all your accumulated knowledge to deal with it.

If you have time to set aside your problems or tasks for a

short while, you may discover that a solution or answer is suddenly found. There is a saying: 'Divine wisdom comes to you while you sleep.' The subconscious mind can find answers which often seem, upon reflection, to be the obvious solution, but which had evaded your conscious mind. You can make it easier for your subconscious mind by clearly defining the problem in your conscious mind and then switching off, letting your subconscious take over and resolve the problem.

4. The Law of Practice

Whatever you do in life, practice is the key to success. The more you practise a musical instrument, the better you will play. The more you practise serving in tennis, the better your serve will be. The more you practise vocabulary in a foreign language, the better you will speak the language.

If you want to get anywhere in life, you must remember two important things: First, you must have the drive or desire to achieve something. Secondly, you must keep practising if you are to succeed. Your input, constant practice, is the price you pay to reach your goal.

5. The Law of Forgiveness

During your life you will learn that anger, resentment, hatred and the desire to bring evil upon others, makes you a weaker person. You lose your equilibrium and perspective as these ugly emotions poison you, tearing you apart. Often these awful feelings do more harm to you than to the person you believe has wronged you.

The simplest solution is to forgive the wrongdoer. This gives you the moral high ground, putting you into a happier frame of mind, and making you feel stronger. You can then move on with your life.

6. The Dual Law of Thought

Each thought you have is made up of two parts: knowledge and emotion. This is similar to the boat analogy, where the rudder is your reason and the sail is your drive.

Your emotions give you power and drive, while your knowledge determines your direction. The amount of knowledge you have doesn't matter on its own, because without the driving force of your emotions, nothing will happen. However if your emotions are very strong but your knowledge is limited, quite a lot may happen, but it can take you in the wrong direction or drive you round in circles. Before following your emotions, you should make sure you also have the necessary knowledge to allow you to decide whether to go down that path.

Your emotional confidence and your belief that you are on the right track are decisive for your life force.

7. The Law of Growth

By dwelling constantly on a particular thought, the more it will grow in your mind. Whether you allow something to grow in importance in your life is up to you. Issues you seldom think about grow smaller and smaller and gradually disappear. Those things you remember and think about often will occupy a larger part of your life.

You have the choice to fill your life with thoughts that are beautiful, pleasant and amusing, or with thoughts that are ugly, dismal and sad.

The quality of your inner, spiritual life depends to a great extent on the thoughts that occupy your mind. It is not the problem itself, but your attitude to the problem, which makes your life onerous and troubled, or happy and fulfilled.

The Bad Deed

Every now and then we all do things that we should not have done. We may have spoiled or broken something and kept quiet about it. We may have taken something that did not belong to us. We may have said something that was not true.

We must learn to deal with these actions, because by themselves they will not go away, but may taint our thoughts and push us off our path.

For example, if you are questioned because you did something wrong, you have two choices.

The first is to lie, in an effort to get out of the situation. An old proverb says, 'Lies have short wings', which means that the questioner is likely to find out what really happened, probably quite quickly. Once they do, you will find yourself trapped in a dead end. And crucially, the person asking the question will have lost confidence in you. Once they find out you have lied, they will lose respect for you and may never trust you again. Trust lost is very hard to regain and many people believe, 'once a liar, always a liar'.

Lying does not offer a solution. Although in the short term it might seem like the easy way out, in the longer term lying serves no good purpose and often causes more damage.

The second choice and best solution is to admit honestly, right at the beginning, what has occurred. In doing so you will win the questioner's trust and he or she will have the choice to either forgive you or punish you. Both these treatments are just and should be acceptable to you.

Often people are not prepared to tell the other party of their own accord, they would rather wait until they are accused. Under these circumstances, the best thing to do is to admit everything at once, and apologise for what happened. It is then up to the hurt party to let matters rest or to punish the wrongdoer as they see fit, the relationship between cause and effect being understood by all concerned.

The Importance of Making a Choice

'Should I read or play ball?'

'Should I do housework or meet with my friends?'

'Should I eat this apple or that biscuit?'

'Shall I take the left road or the right?'

All day we are faced with questions that require us to make a choice. Sometimes the choice is between several possibilities. At this point we have to make a decision.

It is important to know that often these individual choices or decisions do not end there and then. Each option can lead to new possibilities and you may be faced with a chain of choices, decisions and more choices. Consequently, it is important to bear in mind that the possibilities, choices and the decisions you make, all following one another, have an influence on the final result. This eventual outcome may be determined by the very first choice you made.

For this reason it is essential to see clearly your final objective and your desired outcome, as this will help you with your decision-making all the way through.

Therefore, the start of your decision-making is not the

most important thing. It is your focus on the end objective that matters. If you follow your guide beam, and it is clearly aimed at your final objective, this will help you to make the right decisions all the way along your path.

Values

For thousands of years people have lived according to certain values and standards that are prerequisites for a happy and contented personal life, a harmonious family life and a fulfilling community life. Below are twelve values which I believe are essential to this, but there are many more:

- integrity
- diligence
- perseverance
- reliability
- cheerfulness
- punctuality
- zest for learning
- stamina
- obedience
- loyalty
- modesty
- cleanliness

*

You may choose to substitute your own value system for these. Think about each of the values on your list separately and how crucial each of these is to you. Arrange the list according to the importance you attribute to these values by giving each one a number. If, in your opinion, obedience should rank first, mark it with a 1, followed by the next most important value, which should be marked with a 2, until you have evaluated your entire list.

This process allows you to get to know yourself better, which is essential to your development. The ancient Greeks had a temple in Delphi with the following inscription at the gate: 'Know thyself'. Only when you know yourself, your strengths, your weaknesses, your preferences and your dislikes, will you be able to gain sufficient understanding of others and the world around you, and be able to live harmoniously with your environment.

You will find everybody rates their list of values differently. One person may feel that integrity is most important, while perseverance is relatively unimportant. Another may be more interested in punctuality, but feels less inclined towards obedience.

Ask a friend or family member to rank the values on your list and then compare their rankings with yours. You may see that there are fundamental differences between the choices or you may find you are in agreement on many of them. The sequence given allows you to recognise and understand not only your own character and personality, but also that of someone else.

Compatibility with someone can be determined by using this method. For example, if one person places punctuality in third position while the other person places it in eleventh position, it follows that these two people may have problems when they arrange to meet. They may have to find a way to be tolerant of each other's attitude to time-keeping, if they want to avoid conflict.

Groups

There is a well known proverb that dates back to the time of the ancient Greeks. 'Tell me who your friends are and I shall tell you who you are.'

The people who surround us can be divided into groups. For example they can be put into the following categories:
- very clever / of average intelligence / ignorant
- very athletic / somewhat interested in sport / not at all interested in sport
- rich / of average income / poor
- very interested in culture / a bit interested in culture / not at all interested in culture
- hard working / willing to do enough to get by / lazy

The groups of people we associate with are very significant to our lives and have a huge impact on the way we live. Most of us live among a relatively small group of people within a family unit and beyond that we have a fairly small number of close friends. We probably know many more people and may even like quite a few of them, but most of us do not have the time or the inclination to develop really close relationships with more than perhaps 10 people. Even those who claim on social networking sites to have hundreds of friends will most likely only have meaningful relationships with about a dozen.

It is therefore quite natural that we choose our closest friends from certain particular groups. This is where our values play a role. If I am primarily interested in sport, I am likely to prefer to associate with people who are also interested in sport. I may include members from groups that value traits such as loyalty and other compatible values, but I am less likely to find my closest friends among the intelligentsia. Over the years, we attach ourselves to a very specific group of people, who have similar personalities, interests and characteristics as ourselves.

The influences steering us towards membership of certain groups are as follows:

a) You are born with certain characteristics. These include your appearance and your intellectual and entrepreneurial urges, but also your disposition; characteristics such as friendliness, cheerfulness, sociability, laziness, moodiness, and so on.

Most of these characteristics can be influenced and changed throughout your life, some can be eradicated and new ones can be added. It is important to realise that it is up to you to develop your inherent positive character traits in a way that helps you to lead a productive and happy life. Associating with people who have similar positive characteristics can help you to strengthen your own.

b) The herd instinct is the driving force behind the desire to belong to a group. However it is not always easy to gain admittance to a particular set of people, or to be recognised by them as a valuable member. It may require effort from you to achieve this. For example a sports-orientated group might expect you to train a great deal and achieve certain goals in order to become a respected member of their team.

If you start life poor and aspire to be a member of a wealthy group, you will have to work very hard to earn enough money to be admitted to the group.

If you want to associate with a bunch of intellectuals, you need to read a lot, visit museums and art galleries and acquire wide cultural knowledge. Only then will you be of interest to such a coterie.

The earlier in life you know to which group of people you would like to belong, the more systematically you can prepare yourself while you are still young.

Freedom

Nowadays, everybody wants to be 'free'. People want to be free with regard to their faith and religion. They want to be free to develop their talents and their knowledge. They want to be free to work and earn an income and they want to be free to travel, to go to wherever their heart leads them.

In theory, freedom is one of the most precious gifts you may experience in your life. However almost everyone is restricted, in one way or another, from achieving complete freedom. Lack of resources may prevent you from getting a good education. Lack of funds may restrict your movements or prevent you from doing what you would like to do. You may even lack the basics of life, such as sufficient food or good health, which will restrict your choices and your ability to be free.

There are also people who prefer not to have too much freedom. They may not want the responsibility it confers, or perhaps they don't want to have to work as hard as would be necessary to afford the advantages of that freedom.

Being a member of a family or a community, a club or a group, also restricts your freedom. Within a family you will be expected to play a particular role. Within a community compliance with certain rules of conduct will bestow responsibilities onto you.

Nobody is absolutely free.

However to a great extent, it is up to you to decide on the direction your life is going to take and how much freedom you would like to have during your time on Earth. This will depend on the commitment and effort you are prepared to invest in your life.

My father was not willing to accept a professorship at a particular university, as his professional freedom would have suffered. He preferred to keep his independence and his freedom. This made it harder for him to earn a living for his family, but it was the price he was prepared to pay for keeping his professional and intellectual liberty. This freedom was more important to him than income and security.

In all walks of life there are people who value their working independence more than they value a comfortable but restricted existence. You must choose which is more important to you.

Balance and Counterbalance

Most values in life, such as freedom, do not stand alone. Each value is linked to a counter-value. Freedom depends on people abiding by the rules of conduct and the disciplines that apply to groups and societies. The more freedom you wish to have in life, the more disciplined you need to be, to keep a state of balance.

Most characteristics or values in life can be paired with a counter-value. For example:
- passion and reason
- good and evil
- happiness and unhappiness
- warmth and distance
- kindness and hostility
- friendliness and wariness

We are continually placed in situations where we must find a balance between two extremes, e.g. passion versus reason (the sail and the rudder). Depending on the circumstances we are in, we may find we need more reason than passion, or may have to employ more passion than reason, to find a state of equilibrium.

The same rule applies to courage and fear. Courage can be compared to the accelerator in a car. It provides the momentum that propels us forward, towards greater achievements. But without fear acting as a brake, the possibility exists that we could head for disaster. In life, we need both an accelerator and a brake to enable us to follow a steady course towards our objective.

You should try to find a balance between all key life values, because extreme swings in either direction are unsettling.

It is considerably easier to balance these characteristics if you are a member of a group, for example a family, a further education class, a sports club or a local society. Within the confines of the group, you learn to understand values and emotions, sharing sympathy and support, joy and sorrow, success and failure, with the other members.

Understanding and Prudence

As we go through life, whenever we see or experience something new we should try to grasp what is actually taking place. Making sense of what we experience is an essential part of the process of growing up and maturing.

Making sense of things is called understanding. To come to an understanding is an internal process, involving emotion and reason. It is important to remember this before making any decision. Only by taking care to weigh up and balance all factors before making a decision, do we give ourselves the opportunity to understand ourselves and the world in which we live.

Prudence, on the other hand, determines our relationship with all that is happening around us. In the true sense of the word, we have to acquaint ourselves with our environment, whether it's in school or college, on the sports field, on the shop floor, in the office, on the road, or at home. Whatever we do in our daily lives, before doing it we should look around and assess the situation, making sure we fully understand it, and then exercise prudence in our actions.

To a certain extent, prudence also means that we are jointly responsible for other people, to protect them from harm. This means showing compassion and consideration. We are all dependent on the compassion, consideration and prudence of our contemporaries. It is a give and take situation in the truest sense, and illustrates the close relationship between ourselves and others.

This give and take, this relationship between ourselves and others, is linked to the desire and obligation to serve. We were not put onto this Earth to serve only our own needs but also to serve our fellow beings and the natural world. In religion, in voluntary work in our community, and in professions such as nursing and teaching, readiness to serve is considered to be the most precious and noble purpose in life. In contrast is the seeking of self-satisfaction, a modern mannerism that leads to a closed, emotionally unfulfilling and egotistical life.

As a child you may have served by helping your parents, your siblings, your wider family, or your classmates at school. This willingness to help others should continue throughout your life and you will discover the more you do to serve others, the more help you will receive in return.

'As ye have sown, so shall ye reap.'

Physical Health

The saying 'a sound mind in a sound body' dates back to the ancient Romans. Physical health is a prerequisite for a meaningful and rewarding life. This applies to everyone, young, old and all ages in between.

Good health is dependent in part on good food and drink. The body can be likened to an enormous chemical factory which needs not only clean air and clean water, but also the intake of a great many elements such as calcium, magnesium, copper, zinc, potassium, cobalt, iron and so on. If one of these elements is missing, the chemical processes that take place in our bodies cannot happen properly. In other words, we become ill.

There is a well-known rule — the weakest link of a chain determines its strength. The weak point is where the chain will break first. In order to stay healthy it is necessary to eat well-balanced meals that supply the body with all essential elements, so we don't have a 'weak link' in our health. This has become even more important in our modern world. We now know that numerous elements are no longer contained in the soil and consequently the plants and animals that we eat also suffer from a lack of these essential elements. Although our bodies are fairly adaptable, attention should be paid to the foods we eat in terms of their chemical components. You should eat plenty of fresh fruit and vegetables, as these are a good source of elements, as well as the vitamins needed to maintain a healthy body.

Sleep is also vital to keep our bodies healthy. We use a large amount of energy when we are awake, active and busy. Lost energy is restored while we are asleep. If we do not get enough sleep over a period of time we become exhausted, and no longer feel well, strong or efficient. Instead, we become tired, weary and listless. We all react differently to this process of energy restoration. One person may need six hours of sleep to restore lost energy, while another may need nine hours. You will have to find out for yourself how much sleep you need. Young people between the age of 10 and 18, whose bodies are growing and changing, may need a lot more sleep during these years. The growing process requires an enormous amount of energy.

Hygiene too is essential for good health. This includes cleanliness (showering, washing, brushing one's teeth, cleaning and trimming hair and nails) and the regular changing of underclothes.

Finally, sport plays a decisive role too. Physical movement stimulates the blood circulation that is essential for the development of strong and healthy bones and muscles, especially during childhood. However maintaining healthy bones and muscles is of vital importance during our entire lives and during the declining years of old age becomes even more crucial. Keeping active should be an aim for people of all ages.

Time

Time is of special importance to humankind because, of its very nature, it is limited. Each day that passes has 24 hours, no more, no less. The average lifespan measures around 80 years, with a maximum of about 100 years. We cannot bring back time which has passed or take it from tomorrow. Every second of our life is very precious, as it is irreplaceable. It cannot be repeated.

It is therefore very important what we do with our time. We can waste it by sitting around doing nothing useful or constructive. Or we can choose to be active, put effort into any given period of time, increasing the opportunities, experiences and adventures we have during our lifetime. If you want to live an interesting and fulfilling life, you must use every waking hour of the day, to maximise all you can learn and experience.

During school days most of your time is occupied, leaving you little free time during the week, a little more on weekends. The hours you have at your disposal offer various choices: should you be idle and do nothing, or read, engage in sports, play games or maybe spend time with your friends?

Time at school is wasted if you do not pay attention in class. If you concentrate and are studious during lessons, you not only learn, thereby increasing your knowledge, you should also get better marks in your tests and exams. If you don't pay attention, later in your life you may need to use more time to study, to catch up on subject matter you could have learned easily at school.

It is entirely up to you to make the best use of your time.

We all know the expression 'at the right time' and how much can matter. Doing something at the right time can have a very significant effect on the outcome. For example, it would be futile to ask someone to do you a favour if they are under pressure, in a hurry, or in a bad mood. You should wait for the right moment, when they are in a good mood and more receptive — they will be much more inclined to grant your request. Some people have bad timing and often choose the wrong time to do something — consequently they have difficulty achieving their goals. On the other hand, those who are clever (not to say cunning), know to wait for the right moment and this helps them to be successful.

Depending on the circumstances sometimes one should

act quickly, seizing the moment, while at other times it is better to be patient and wait. It is not easy to acquire a good sense of time and timing. However, you should know that time and the flow of it are of crucial importance to success. It can be very disappointing to miss the right time in a matter of importance, where the timing affects the outcome.

In order to further understand the concept of time and the use of it, try to keep an hourly record of how you spent your time for four consecutive weekends. If you add up all the hours spent on each activity, you will discover how little, or perhaps how much, you actually achieved. In this way you can see how much time passed without you making good use of it.

Remember: Time is of the Essence.

Annual Inventory

Towards the end of each year, or perhaps if you are studying, at the end of the academic year, pause for an hour and make an inventory by asking yourself the following:

1. What have I learnt during the last year with regard to the way I live my life?
2. What did I do well? What could I have done better?
3. What are my resolutions for the coming year?

Write your answers down, because this will help you in your commitment towards what you hope to achieve over the next year.

This is a useful exercise for people of any age, and can be done by children as well as by adults. Below is a list containing some resolutions made by my son when he was 10 years old:

1. Practise if something does not work well
2. Use time more purposefully

3. Ambition, to be in front

4. Read at least two books a month

5. Form my own opinion, do not follow the crowd

6. Develop inherited and my own characteristics

7. Common sense

8. Concentrate and control my thoughts.

My daughter, at the age of 12, was more precise: she compiled a daily timetable that showed she wanted to sleep for eight hours, spent two hours eating and on personal hygiene, and allocated 10 hours for attending school and doing home work. This left her with four hours a day at her disposal. One hour was earmarked for reading and three hours were reserved for playing. She intended to do something every day to promote her own future and, above all, to be a winner through hard work, practice and concentration. She was already aware of the fact that it takes hard work to be successful.

Efficient, diligent people, through their positive attitudes and hard work, create the basis for success. Non-achievers often see success as a stroke of luck bestowed from heaven, but there is no substitute for hard work.

Cause and Effect

'Great oaks from little acorns grow.'

Everything that happens to you in your life has a reason, or cause. The reason is often something within your control, such as your attitude, your way of thinking, or your actions.

If you drop litter on the pathway (cause), you may have been the reason that someone trips and breaks a leg (effect). If you look in the wrong direction before crossing the road (cause), you could be hit by a vehicle (effect).

It is sometimes useful to look at something that happens (the effect) and trace your steps back to find the reason (the cause). If you do a piece of work badly, you might ask yourself why. What was the cause? Perhaps you did not prepare well enough, or you did not concentrate while doing it? Maybe you jotted your notes down in a hurry, or you did not think matters through carefully? A sloppy attitude towards work (cause) will almost certainly produce bad results (effect).

Cause and effect create a chain reaction whereby

something can produce an effect that may be the reason for a further happening, and so on. For example, a factory may produce toxic waste (cause) that is disposed of in a river. This in turn results in fish being poisoned or dying (effect). If the fish are poisonous (cause) and subsequently eaten by humans (effect), the original cause (the toxic waste) leads not only to the poisoning of fish (effect), it is also the cause for the poisoning of humans (effect).

When something unexpected or unwanted happens in our lives, we often ask ourselves why. In other words, when something unpleasant is happening to us, it can be helpful to ascertain the cause. We need to find out the reason to understand fully what is happening to us. Once we understand, it may be possible to put things right.

For example, if someone behaves in an unfriendly or hostile way towards you, you should try to discover why. When you have done this, you may be able to change your attitude or behaviour in such a way that the person concerned treats you in a friendly manner again.

Cause and Effect in Relation to Life

Many people believe that a divine being (or God) controls our lives. However, one may also be of the opinion that the opposite is true, and that each of us is in control of our own destiny. The Scriptures tell us that Man has been assigned to create his own environment and according to the Bible we are each responsible for what happens to us and to our surroundings. Each person controls their own life and living conditions by the nature of their mental disposition, which they themselves can determine. A person's environment is created, to a very great extent, by their attitude, their actions and their faith.

You may have trust in the future because things are going well, but bear in mind that things may be going well because you have trust in the future.

You determine how you live each day. If, when you wake in the morning, you tell yourself 'It's going to be a wonderful day,' it will probably become a wonderful day — your positive attitude will help determine it. If you do not say this to yourself, your mind will not know what to expect of the new day, and it may not turn out so well.

You alone are the controller of your thoughts, so you alone determine the way you look at each new day and at your environment. If you put yourself into a happy mood, you will see cheerful and happy things. If you are in a bad mood, everything will seem dreary and sad.

Life is what you make it!

Prayers are so important because this is when (with a little dose of common sense) you tell your mind and your soul what you would like to happen. In this way you are telling your mind and soul what matters to you and what to concentrate on. You are a tiny part of a divine being, which will help you to conduct yourself in such a way that you can achieve what you desire.

Quantity and Quality

When we talk of quantity we mean volume, the mass or amount of something. When we talk of quality, we mean the nature or attributes of something.

Although these two terms differ considerably in meaning, they are intertwined — one cannot exist without the other. A quantity of something will always have a quality.

The quality of our possessions and our surroundings is much more important than the quantity (in the sense of how big, grand or impressive). There are people who talk a lot (high quantity) but have nothing to say that is of value (poor quality). Someone else may utter only one sentence (small quantity) that bears a much more worthwhile meaning (high quality). Quality is much more important than quantity.

There are a few instances when the opposite may be true. There are obvious advantages to having more rather than less money. And in certain circumstances, for example where food is concerned, the quantity or amount available to eat can be as important as the quality — someone who is starving will not care about the quality, just whether they are getting sufficient food to survive. In this instance, quality and quantity are closely related.

But generally speaking, quality is much more important than quantity.

One true and loyal friend can be much more valuable to you than dozens of acquaintances.

One quality item of clothing can bring more joy and last much longer than ten items of inferior quality.

One good book can be more enriching and enlightening than a dozen pulp novels.

One beautiful rose can bring more happiness than an entire bunch of flowers.

Your guiding principle should be to concentrate on quality rather than quantity.

Trust

The relationship between two people is fundamentally determined by mutual trust. Mutual trust entails an absolute reliance on one another.

What you say is important. There is a proverb that says: 'A man is as good as his word.' It means that the other person can rely absolutely on what you are saying.

A promise you make should be the equivalent to you having done whatever you promised to do — in effect, a guarantee.

Expressions such as, 'I'll see what I can do,' or 'I'm not sure whether it can be done,' illustrate a lack of commitment and mean nothing.

Trust also includes accuracy and punctuality. Any type of untidiness and carelessness, sloppiness or a nonchalant attitude, can be detrimental to developing trust.

Whether you win a person's trust or not depends on what you actually say, and more importantly what you do, over a long period of time.

Once you have won a person's trust, the slightest

misconduct, such as telling a lie, can abruptly and effectively destroy that trust. It is often impossible to regain trust. If someone has lost their faith in you, they may never trust you again.

Trust is perhaps the greatest of all values. People will only commit themselves fully and wholeheartedly to those they trust.

The Moment of Mental Resistance

Working, taking part in sport, even listening to a lecture, all require an effort and at some point, a moment of mental resistance will be reached. 'I'm getting tired or bored... my energy and my enthusiasm are deteriorating... I would prefer to stop what I am doing and move on to something else.'

When you become aware of reaching this point, you need to take yourself in hand, as you are actually able to continue for much longer. If you keep going you will find that after a while you will reach another point of resistance, and whether you overcome this one or not will depend entirely on you and your endurance, both physical and mental.

Think of something you have to do which requires practice, such as playing a musical instrument, or improving your serve in tennis. You decide to practise your tennis and after about thirty serves, during which your service actually improves slightly, you reach the first point of resistance. You are a bit bored and would like to stop there and then. But you know that it would be beneficial to continue with another thirty practice serves.

Your mind (which is telling you it would be good to keep going) has little power and determination at this moment, because your emotions (which are telling you to stop) are more powerful in this situation.

However, if you can reactivate your emotional commitment to the task, by giving yourself a good reason to keep going, you will find this stimulates your energy levels sufficiently for you to practise thirty more serves (which will certainly improve the quality of your tennis).

No doubt you will reach another point of resistance and again be tempted to give up. Your mind knows that you should practise your serve 100 times per session to make a real improvement. It is up to you to stimulate your emotional energy each time you hit this moment of resistance, enabling you to continue practising until you have reached your goal.

Most people do not get past the first moment of resistance and consequently remain mediocre players. They will never become really good tennis players (or musicians, or skilled at anything), as they don't have the dedication required to overcome the points of resistance. Without this determination, they will never be better than average.

People can achieve considerably more than they think they can. During sports training or P.E. you might believe you can't go on any longer, and feel you have reached your point of exhaustion. Since you are forced by the trainer or coach to continue, you have to keep going. Half an hour later, you will reach the same point, and you may still be made to go on. Finally, you will realise that you achieved four times as much as you believed you were capable of.

Remember — your body stores an enormous amount of energy and has vast reserves, but it is your mind that determines to what extent you use these.

Being an Entrepreneur

Anybody who works independently is an entrepreneur.

Many people do not want to be entrepreneurs, because self-employment requires effort and may bring problems that they are not prepared to endure. These people may shy away from responsibilities and are usually content to do as they are told. Though this may not always be very pleasant, they do not have to carry the burden of success or failure (with the obvious exception that they are responsible for their own individual work). Their future working life is normally assured by their employer.

It follows that in order to lead an independent business life, you have to meet certain requirements. First of all, there are certain values that are necessary, such as self-confidence, trust in your reliability, awareness of your responsibilities towards customers and clients and a strong drive to succeed. It requires great emotional strength to realise your own ambitions and goals. Hence, a strong faith in yourself, a good knowledge of your chosen business and considerable stamina are needed to overcome all those points of resistance that will confront you. A single-minded vision is needed to help you reach your goal. That goal must be clearly defined and you must focus all your energy onto it, like a laser beam, to develop the necessary stamina. If your energies are dissipated in many directions, much more time will be needed to reach your ultimate target.

It is essential to have the right attitude towards hard work. A successful entrepreneur not only works hard, but generally works much longer hours than his or her employees. While an employee may have time for activities outside work, a successful entrepreneur will probably be busy day and night thinking about business problems and the development of the business. Time for leisure activities may not be available or may have to be scheduled into the work diary.

Furthermore, an entrepreneur has to be extremely careful with his or her financial resources. An entrepreneur carries the risks alone. If insufficient funds are available to keep the business going, it may be forced to close down, leaving not only the owner of the business out of work, but also any employees.

Many creative people such as artists have a difficult life in this respect. In the past they were often made to feel like beggars, because their patrons expected much from them, without being prepared to provide the funds necessary for them to continue with their work. Earning a living is still very hard today for many writers, artists and musicians and requires a lot of passion, commitment and dedication.

Being an entrepreneur requires particular values too: vision, faith in your ability, drive and stamina.

However, if you are successful, the rewards can be high. The investment in your abilities and your complete commitment to the job will give you the freedom to create your own life and be in control of your own fate.

Rights and Responsibilities

Nowadays people talk a lot about rights: human rights; the rights of the individual; the rights of women, of children, of animals, and so on. There was a time, years ago, when people were much more aware of responsibilities rather than rights. However, in this day and age, responsibilities are seldom discussed, although rights and responsibilities go hand in hand.

For example, if your parents found the money to send you to a good private school, or helped support you through university to give you a first-class education, it was your responsibility to work hard and make the best use of your education. All children have the right to an education, but it means nothing if they do not feel it is their responsibility to do their best to benefit from this education.

Moreover, for many years parents do everything they can to make their children capable of taking charge of their own lives. It follows therefore that (whether one likes it or not), there is a certain obligation, a responsibility, to look after one's parents when they are old and no longer in a position to earn a living, and to make their lives as comfortable as possible.

Every single one of us has a responsibility to help others in our families and in our neighbourhoods, and to contribute to the political and sociological development of our communities, to support poor, needy and sick people, and to do everything possible to help care for and maintain the world around us.

One could be of the opinion that responsibilities should take precedence over rights. Rights should not be taken for granted, rather they should be regarded as a privilege, to be earned. We earn them by carrying out our responsibilities — and receive them in return for our contribution to the world in which we live.

Personality

Personality describes the impression people make on each other. You make an impression on others even before you speak, however what you say and how you say it hugely enhances the impact of your personality.

Some people have a very strong personality, with a lot of influence on others, while many people have relatively little charisma. Some people make hardly any impression at all on others.

The impact a person makes through their personality can affect different people in different ways, depending on their own personality and the relationship between them. Someone may radiate self-confidence, appearing experienced and assured. This may give people confidence in them, but if these qualities are exaggerated, some people may feel intimidated.

There are people who radiate so much love and kindness that others feel safe, comfortable and reassured in their presence.

Other people have personalities that simply emit their

love for life — they are always cheerful, probably starting every morning believing that the day ahead will be a great day. This positive attitude affects the people around them, who in turn feel stimulated and encouraged to be upbeat and optimistic.

The impact we have on others through the appearance and effect of our personality mirrors our spiritual and mental frame of mind, a state largely determined by ourselves. After all, we are in control of our thoughts that, to a large degree, influence our emotions.

In this way, it follows that our personality and the effect it has on others is very much something within our own control.

The Principle of Efficiency

'As ye sow, so shall ye reap.'

You may remember this phrase in connection with serving others, but it is relevant to your own welfare, too. It means that you need to do something (sow), before you can be rewarded for your efforts (reap). The same rule applies to your earnings. You must work to achieve something before you can receive payment for it.

It is important to remember that you will always receive fair remuneration for your work, although it may take some time. If your employer does not pay enough, another employer may offer you more money, either because he or she places a higher value on your work, or is a more generous person. It follows that you should not fret too much about the amount of income you receive. You should primarily concentrate on the quality of your work — remember that the harder you work and more efficient you are, the higher your income will eventually be.

Nowadays you need to learn and study throughout your life, becoming more efficient, more knowledgeable and more competent as you get older. The global body of human knowledge is constantly being expanded as scientists, researchers and inventors add to it, so it is essential that you keep yourself informed and up to date with developments in your line of work, so you can remain competitive and able to offer work of the highest calibre. You can learn by reading on the internet or from books about areas which are of interest to your sphere of activity. That way you can follow the latest developments from all over the world.

It is of paramount importance to use your time sensibly, because there is so much to learn. For example, you could try to learn another language or even two — it might be hugely beneficial to your career if you could converse well not only in English, but also French or German, Russian or Spanish, as these are important languages spoken all over the world. People who can speak Arabic or Chinese are highly sought after as employees in many parts of the world.

Decide on your priorities and choose the languages that will be most useful to your work, so you can make the best use of your time.

Style

In the same way that an artist may work in several different styles, a person may live their life in a variety of different styles.

Let us start with language. Some people use very ordinary language. They may have a relatively limited vocabulary and may swear a lot. Others, who are educated and well read, may have a far greater vocabulary and prefer not to use offensive language. You may choose to use slightly different language depending on the company you are with. You might use more formal language when you are with your family, particularly older members, and more informal, casual language with your friends.

The same applies to clothing. In the business world people are usually expected to dress in quite a formal way. In most financial centres the majority of men wear a dark suit, a light-coloured shirt and a tie. Women in this environment are expected to wear skirts of a moderate length, to dress plainly and to hide their femininity to some extent. Conservative clothing is the norm in many business, political, legal and financial institutions.

In other professional areas, for example the media and creative industries, less conventional, more colourful clothing is acceptable and is often seen as an expression of an employee's personality.

The same applies to hairstyles. In many work places men are expected to have short hair and be clean-shaven, which is seen as a symbol of neatness and good personal hygiene. However with some professionals, for example artists, designers, and computer experts, individual talents and abilities are considered to be far more essential than appearance. In these occupations, length of hair and style of clothing is not regarded as important.

So depending on the restrictions within your working environment and your own taste, you will gradually develop your own style.

Often, style and taste are seen as the expression of a personal discipline, an inner order (or disorder). Someone who is outwardly neat and tidy and speaks eloquently is unlikely to be untidy in his or her way of thinking or living. On the other hand, you cannot readily assume that a person who looks untidy or uses improper language is less talented or less efficient. They simply may not care about such things and feel they are trivial.

Style and taste also depend to some extent on your education, your background, your personal aesthetic sense and, of course, on your financial resources. Rich people can have designer-made suits or dresses, while poorer people have to buy what they can afford, rather than what they might want.

Personal style and taste also influence your choice of the people you socialise with and feel comfortable among. Generally, they will be people who like what you like, and behave in the same way as you do yourself.

You are Always a Sales Person

As soon as you meet another person you are selling something. Either you want to make a good impression, in which case you are selling yourself, or perhaps you are trying to sell them an idea or a product. You should always remember that you, and what you are selling, will be continuously assessed by others, which can have a huge impact on your position in life or within a certain environment.

In a business sales situation, it is best to relax and behave as naturally as possible. Many people pretend to be somebody they would like to be, rather than being themselves. Although their deception is not always obvious immediately, disappointment is unavoidable at a later stage, because they will be unable to fulfil expectations they have raised, or to accomplish tasks they gave the impression they could do. It is always better to be honest about yourself right from the start, rather than pretending to be what you are not.

You may have heard about 'hard' and 'soft' selling

methods. If you push aggressively to sell an idea or a product (hard selling), this may make a strong impression initially, but the buyer may find this approach intimidating, distasteful and even repellent and ultimately be put off. Soft selling, which includes being honest and friendly and not exaggerating, always makes a better impression and is more likely to be successful, especially in building long term business relationships.

There are people who love selling and excel at it and consequently are successful in business. Others do not like selling, finding it hard — they should choose a profession which does not involve trying to convince others to buy something. However persuasive language, self-confidence and the ability to sell yourself to others are key ingredients for success not only in business but in much of what we do through life.

Selling is an art that can be acquired to a certain degree. Many Americans are specialists in the art of selling — their entrepreneurial culture encourages the development of this skill. They have strong ideas that they try to sell softly, and in this they are often very successful throughout the world.

The talent to lead others also requires good selling skills. Successful leaders employ these skills by using soft selling, drawing people along with them. If they are skilled at this, it is much more effective than hard selling. The soft sell uses the energy of the audience to motivate themselves, while the hard sell uses the energy of the seller and is akin to trying to push people into doing something.

The Law of Compensation

It is a universal law that the sum total of all energy in the cosmos, and consequently the total amount of energy on Earth, remains constant. If an amount of energy accumulates in one place, it has been taken from somewhere else. Energy cannot disappear or get lost — it always exists in some form or other, and a state of balance is always restored.

All matter consists of energy. Matter means any substance that has a mass and therefore occupies space, (as opposed to something mental or spiritual). It therefore follows that you consist of energy.

Everything that happens is offset by another happening — all activity is compensated for. Every action results in a reaction, and this applies not only to physical activity but also to spiritual activity:

- an input leads to an output
- an attitude leads to a counter-attitude or appropriate response
- if you give love, you will receive love in return

– saving is offset against spending

This Law of Compensation should lead you to various conclusions:

1. Nothing in life is free. Even the receipt of a gift should generate gratitude (unless it is in repayment for an obligation from the giver).
2. You cannot take back what has been said. Once something has been spoken there will be a reaction (good or bad) and you can't take back what was said without causing a further reaction, so think before you speak.
3. True coincidences are very rare. A situation is created by your attitude and the attitudes of others, your actions and the actions of others. A situation may erroneously be described as a coincidence, but nothing happens without a reason.

There are basically two types of people. Some people generate relatively little energy. They are placid and passive and react less obviously to external circumstances or stimulation. They show little sign of physical activity, although they may be very thoughtful and contemplative.

Other people generate a lot of energy. They are active and physical, promoting creativity within their environment and encouraging and stimulating others.

These two types of people balance out each other, compensating for their differences, and both types are essential for a balanced society. If you understand the compensatory process and its effects on you, you will better be able to understand what is happening within yourself, the people around you and the world in which you live.

Broad-mindedness and Narrow-mindedness

People can have a broad mind, an average mind, or a narrow mind.

To be broad-minded means you have wide knowledge and an open mind. You are interested in the arts, science, music, literature, psychology, all aspects of your business, cultural and social lives. You think about life and all it entails. You will have read and seen much and used that knowledge and your experiences to look for the relationship between them. This further broadens your mind enabling you to understand life better. An open mind is receptive to new ideas.

Narrow-mindedness is exactly the opposite. A person with a narrow mind is interested in only a few subjects and is unconcerned about acquiring knowledge and new ideas. He or she is not interested in broadening their mind. A narrow-minded person has fixed ideas and does not want to change them.

However, having a broad mind is not necessarily a prerequisite for a happy life. On the contrary, it is possible that a narrow-minded person can find their place in life much more easily than a person with an enquiring mind, and hence can lead a simple but happy life, comfortable with their lot. A broad-minded person may spend time soul-searching, looking for meaning and fulfilment in many different directions, which can lead to dissatisfaction and disappointment.

It is important to understand that a broad-minded person can narrow their mind for certain purposes. If you are interested in many things you have to distribute your energy in many different directions. Consequently, only a small portion of your energy can be directed towards each of these interests. If, on the other hand, in order to reach a certain goal you concentrate on only one issue, you combine all your energy, thereby consciously narrowing your mind. This is called focusing and it concentrates your energies and thoughts in one direction, rather like a laser beam. This can be essential if you are to achieve a successful outcome.

On the other hand, it takes many years to broaden a narrow mind. It can be done by reading extensively, listening to other people and, crucially, by being open and receptive to new thoughts and ideas. Under normal circumstances your mind is initially broadened by your parents, your education, your environment and above all by you taking an interest in learning. What you have not learnt during your first 20 years will be more difficult to make up for in later years. As an adult you have to absorb new ideas and experiences constantly and have less time for formal education, so taking in new knowledge, for example by learning a language, will be that much harder.

However all of life is a learning process, so make use of your time wisely and be open to new ideas and experiences throughout your life.

The Truth

Knowledge of 'real' truth is something we humans are unable to achieve. Everything we know – our entire thinking and perception – is determined by our inherent characteristics, our upbringing and our experiences. The combination of these factors results in each of us developing our own individual state of mind, which in turn means each of us perceives everything we know from a personal point of view. Everybody sees, understands and interprets themselves and the rest of the world purely from their own viewpoint, that is, subjectively.

However from time to time, it is important to make an effort to see the truth accurately, and this means trying to look at something objectively. You can do this by examining an event or fact from a different point of view than your own. In other words, look at it from someone else's viewpoint. Such a procedure allows you to put your own subjective perception behind you, and to scrutinise something without allowing your emotions or prejudices to influence your viewpoint. In this way, you can look at something as objectively as possible — you may find you come to a different conclusion than you would have viewing the same thing subjectively.

This technique of using objectivity to view something has the added advantage that several people, even quite a large number, can attempt an objective appraisal of something by examining the facts together from a similar viewpoint.

It is very important to remember that everything you see or hear is perceived through your own eyes and ears, so you should be very careful before offering a personal opinion or judgment. You must not forget that each of us conditions our own mind, which in turn determines how each of us looks at the world.

Trying to look at a situation objectively is critical for achieving a clear and truthful understanding of the world around you and also for helping to develop your ability to get on with others.

The Law of Diminishing Returns

When you first eat a piece of chocolate you will probably enjoy it tremendously. When you eat a second piece, it still tastes good, but not as good as the first piece. If you continue eating, you will probably discover that further pieces of chocolate give you less satisfaction and by the time you have eaten the whole bar or finished the box, it is nothing special any more.

This is called the law of diminishing returns and you can apply it to many areas of life.

If you go on a family treat to a theme park once a year, it becomes a very special occasion that you look forward to, and probably remember with joy. If you went once a month, it would become rather a routine event, and if you went every week, you would soon become bored with it.

If you party once a month it may give you great pleasure. If you party every week, it is still fine, though may feel less special. If you party every day, it will become routine and insignificant, and may even become unbearable.

Often, the more we have of something, the less we value and appreciate it.

As with so many of life's pleasures, you will realise that it is the quality of something, not the quantity, which determines your degree of enjoyment and the value you place on it.

In a Foreign Country

In the same way that you have developed your own attitude and a point of view through which you perceive everything around you, the people within your neighbourhood, city and country, will have done the same.

Inhabitants of other countries will also have done this. They will speak their own languages and follow their own customs and ways of living. They may think about issues and see things in ways that are completely different from the way you, the people in your environment and in your country, see and think about the world.

In order to understand this, it makes sense when you are in a foreign country to allow your own way of thinking and your own opinions to take a back seat. That way, after a while in a foreign environment, you may learn about the habits of other people and perhaps discover interesting differences between their way of thinking and your own.

Although it may require a bit of effort, if you are spending time in another country it makes sense to adapt to the way of living and the attitudes of the indigenous population. Maintaining or insisting on continuing with your own way of living may provoke a defensive response from local people and it will certainly not be conducive to mutual efforts to understand one another. Pushing or hard selling of your own ideas and beliefs is not advisable. Instead, try to adapt and fit in, showing respect for the local way of life.

If you are patient and show you are trying to adjust to their way of living, it is possible that local residents may become inquisitive about you, and may even try to find out about your life and your way of thinking. This would be the right moment to tell them, humbly and discreetly, about things that you may consider would interest them. This soft approach is much more likely to be successful and to achieve mutual respect between you and the people of your host country.

Right from the beginning you should take into consideration that time, and the perception of time, can differ from country to country. For example, punctuality is generally not considered to be particularly important in Brazil, which can be quite stressful for someone who is always punctual. He or she may find it impossible to live there, as they are constantly stressed by the lack of accurate timekeeping. By comparison, in much of the

Arabian world, people who are tardy and forever rushing about are considered uncultured, and being hasty is not seen as an acceptable way to behave.

In some countries there are also major cultural differences between the way men and women are expected to behave, often because of religious observances. It is very important to be aware of these and abide by them in a respectful way.

When you are in a foreign country, be friendly and receptive, respectful of local laws and customs, and try to keep a low profile.

The Conscious Mind, the Subconscious Mind and Intuition

I have already explained that you can broaden both your conscious and your subconscious mind by reading and experiencing as much as possible. In this way you can widen your horizons.

You will also know that your subconscious mind has accumulated and stored everything your brain and senses have experienced throughout your life and is therefore a treasure trove of knowledge. If you have a problem, your subconscious mind will be working on it, in order to help your conscious mind find a solution. As the subconscious mind uses all its knowledge, it cannot act according to your perception of time, it has to follow its own course. So the best thing is to do is relax and wait until your subconscious mind has found an answer. This may come to you while you are sleeping, but is nevertheless conclusive and a valid solution.

In addition to our conscious and subconscious minds, we also have intuition. This is best described as a feeling, and is connected not only with the subconscious mind but also to forces beyond our conscious minds and our senses.

You will know that your five primary senses, (touch, taste, smell, hearing, seeing), perceive only some of the forces or dynamic influences of the natural world. We have learned from studying the natural world that many animals instinctively respond to forces that we humans do not consciously react to, such as the Earth's magnetic pull, weather patterns, seasonal changes, parental imprinting and circadian rhythms, even radar and similar forces that we humans cannot detect. However you may be aware unconsciously of forces such as these, and your instinctive reaction to these forces can be called intuition or common sense.

We cannot plan for the future by the use of common sense alone. Often you cannot rely on your common sense to understand the course your life takes, but if you have a good relationship with your intuition, it can help guide you towards what is best. Playing with possibilities and using your imagination may only lead you to consider limited alternatives to guide you on your future course. People with good instincts and well-developed intuition may instinctively know the best course to follow. This intuition is often more highly developed in very sensitive people and generally more women than men possess good intuition, but it can be cultivated and stimulated in anyone, especially by taking an interest in those areas of culture that encourage the imagination and creative thinking, such as art, music and the theatre.

We therefore have three systems at our disposal to help us in our decision-making: our conscious mind, comprising intellect and emotions; our subconscious mind; and our intuition. All of these can assist us in making good decisions and choosing the right path through life.

Finding Your Own Course

If you are trying to gain a good understanding of what is happening within yourself and within your environment, it often helps if you search for new knowledge and new experiences.

The Scriptures tell us, 'Seek and you shall find.' If you are a seeker, you will knock at many doors, some of which will be opened to you, inviting you in to explore unknown worlds, learn new things and add to your experiences. If you only knock every now and then, or even not at all, no doors will be opened for you, and your path to understanding yourself and the world around you will be much harder.

If you seek out new experiences, you can then draw upon the wisdom of others and learn life rules which have been valid for thousands of years, and these will help you along your own path. Doubtless, everything you discover will have been experienced by thousands before you, but in the final analysis, it is up to you to decide which experiences and rules are of significance and applicable to you, to your life, and to your own course.

In this way you may gradually develop into a personality with a distinct and individual profile, recognised by others as such.

It is important to be honest and true to yourself and to act accordingly. It makes no sense to pretend to be somebody else, or to follow a course that is alien to you. Perhaps you don't have the prerequisites that made another person follow this particular course. You must find your own path.

You will become stronger mentally and a more unique and distinct person if you always stay true to yourself. Follow your own path, so at the end of your life you will be able to say (or even sing), 'I did it *my* way.'

The Soul

Many people, from many different religions, believe each person has a soul that is part of the Almighty, or a divine being. Some people talk about there being an endless sea of souls. I believe each of us is part of that sea and consequently a part of eternity.

Many philosophers and religions also believe that our souls travel through a multitude of lives — we have all experienced a series of previous lives and can look forward to many more after this one. They believe that our souls, during the course of their many lives, are in the process of maturing and developing, and during the course of each life, each soul will make a decision about how best to move towards its final objective, the state of being reunited with the Almighty.

The idea of the progress of the soul can also be looked at from the viewpoint of atonement. Many great poets, such as Goethe, support the theory that if you have suffered greatly during this life or have tried to lead a virtuous existence, you will go to heaven.

In other words, a compensatory process will take place during your next life, relative to what happens to you in this life.

You could also assume that a happy, successful and fulfilled life may prompt the soul to seek a certain amount of grief during the next life, to continue the process of development and maturing.

The existence and nature of the human soul has kept many religions and a huge number of philosophers and religious thinkers occupied for thousands of years, because there have been, without doubt, indications of the existence of previous lives in some people.

Since each person's soul is part of a larger, infinite group of souls, it should be assumed that this affects the subconscious mind, as well as one's intuition. The subconscious mind may contain stored experiences of previous lives, and that may influence both your subconscious thought processes and your intuition.

Old and New Values

In the Western world the old order of values, that had been established for centuries, was severely disrupted during the 20th century by two world wars. These were followed in the second half of the 20th century by the rapid rise of consumerism and huge increases in communication and globalisation, with the effect that during the last fifty years humans as individuals assumed an importance never before seen. The interests of the church, of nations, of communities and even of families, were often ignored, replaced by the self-satisfaction of the individual as the highest goal. This trend considerably reduced the number of churchgoers in many developed countries and also reduced people's commitment to their community. Egoism – interest in oneself – took priority over everything else. Even the future of the family unit was threatened, as divorce and new forms of cohabitation became acceptable.

The development of a consumerist society and the idea that everything we do must be for personal gain became the order of the day. Obligations and responsibilities were observed only to a limited degree and many of the old values that had been a crucial part of the fabric of society for centuries lost their significance and meaning.

As a result of these changes, many people felt they had lost their way, no longer able to rely on the traditional framework of values and relationships to underpin their lives and give them meaning.

To date there is no sign of a new structure being created to replace what has been lost and consequently large numbers of people are living increasingly lonely lives. Many people are looking for a vision or message that can unite them with their neighbours and communities, binding them together through a common goal or belief. However these gatherings are rare and are often disrupted by the political motivation of some people at these meetings, which can cause unrest and division.

Without this external framework to guide us and give our lives structure, it has become necessary for each of us to create our own personal order of values, priorities and commitments to underpin us. These values should not be governed exclusively by our individual preferences and desires, but should include the concept of commitment towards families, groups, communities and our own culture. This will not happen automatically, it requires great effort and commitment and also an environment that can nourish specific goals and specific life styles. Once this framework is in place in the larger community, it will provide guidelines for us and for others.

Masculine and Feminine Characteristics

In this section I have used very broad generalisations referring to masculine and feminine characteristics. These are based on the fact that in ancient times, each sex had a very defined role that helped to ensure the survival of the species. Cave women gathered food near the home and cared for the children, while cave men hunted. Nowadays, masculine and feminine roles encompass a far wider variety of characteristics, but for the sake of simplicity and clarity, I am using very traditional terms of reference here.

Everybody has both masculine and feminine characteristics. Historically, masculine features would be seen as strength and courage, the instinct to hunt and to fight, the need for authority and, to a lesser extent, a degree of boorishness and a lack of consideration for the needs of others. Feminine traits would include emotional empathy, maternal and caring instincts, gentleness and a sensitivity to the feelings of others.

A blend of both masculine and feminine characteristics can be found in everybody, determined in varying degrees by genetic inheritance, the effect of a person's upbringing, and the presence of masculine and feminine hormones in the body. Depending on the mix of all these factors, the results are hugely varied, and may produce men with very masculine traits, men with feminine characteristics, and men who have a balance of both. Conversely, there are very feminine women, women who display masculine traits, and women who show a mix of both.

In order to understand people, you have to understand that everyone has this blend of masculine and feminine characteristics, particularly as sexual preferences and attitudes often depend on them.

In addition to these sexual characteristics, your personality is also affected by the way your brain deals with the world. The brain is made up of two hemispheres, the right and the left. The right hemisphere controls the left side of the body and processes information from the left eye. In the majority of people this side also controls creativity and intuition, is more responsive to art, music and has a strong visual sense. The left hemisphere of the brain controls the right side of the body and processes information from the right eye. In most people this side of the brain is more logical and analytical, with a strong verbal sense. However, while certain types of tasks and thinking tend to be associated with a particular area of the brain, no one is fully 'right-brained' or 'left-brained' and most people do better at tasks when the entire brain is utilised. It is important for everyone to try and use both sides of their brain, engaging their masculine and feminine traits and their logical/analytical and creative sides.

Expectations

Everybody has certain expectations in life, as well as in their day to day living. Each step we take, all our actions, everything we talk about, is done in relation to our expectations of the outcome of our actions or our words. Hence the way these expectations are formulated is very important.

If your expectations are too high or you do something that makes their realisation impossible, you must prepare yourself for disappointment. However you do not have to take such risks if your expectations are moderate. If you have reasonable expectations, you can live in harmony with the outcome.

You yourself can determine what you expect of your life. As your mind and your attitude will determine your adult environment to a large degree, you need to get to know yourself well. First and foremost you need to know:
- your mental strengths and weaknesses
- your physical strengths and weaknesses
- the state and potential of your abilities

- your sensitivities
- the relationship between your passions and your mental strength
- the relative importance of your values, both now and in the future

These characteristics differ hugely from person to person and you have to adapt yourself accordingly to achieve compatibility with others. If you share your life with another person and perhaps have a family, you will need to make sure you all respect each other's expectations, and accept and adapt if these differ from your own.

It follows that expectations, and in particular your ambitions, should be kept within the framework of your own characteristics and personality, as well as your living circumstances.

You also should understand and accept that, although you may be able to slow it down by living healthily, you cannot stop the gradual ageing and disintegration of your body and ultimately its death (though from a spiritual point of view, your eternal soul may live for ever).

The Meaning of Intention

It is important to know that the development of thoughts and emotions begins with an intention formed in your subconscious mind. We already know that our subconscious is intensely occupied with absorbing everything our mind, our senses and our soul experiences. The assimilation of all these experiences may result in the development of certain intentions. Without being aware of it, your subconscious may already have the intention to bring a certain activity to an end, or to give preference to something, or to change this or that with regard to your relationships with others.

It is interesting that although your conscious mind will still follow its usual behavioural pattern, your attitude will subconsciously reflect these intentions and this may become obvious to others. In that situation it follows that everything you do or say to others may no longer appear sincere and people may suspect you of having what is sometimes called a 'hidden agenda'. This often gives rise to the question of what you are really trying to achieve and what your real intentions are.

This may prompt you to question yourself, by examining what your intentions really are, in order to establish a clear, open and honest attitude.

It is helpful to be familiar with this process in order to understand indecisiveness in others, and why their attitude may no longer appear to be clear and true, but indistinct and even confused. They may be trying to give the appearance of following conscious motivations, while actually following subconscious intentions. If you show understanding rather than being suspicious, you may be able to help them find their way back to their own desired path.

Risk

Everything you do involves a certain risk, even just talking to another person. For example, they may misunderstand you because you don't articulate clearly. Whenever we express ourselves, we take the risk that others will not understand our meaning.

The same applies to your entire attitude. You may unintentionally overlook somebody, or offend somebody, or may do something which causes a reaction that is totally different from what you expected.

We are constantly faced with situations full of these risks, which may be considered to be small and unimportant. However, these seemingly insignificant occurrences can have huge consequences. You might say something utterly stupid that will be remembered by someone else for many years. It could have been something totally inappropriate, shocking the other person to such an extent that it is impossible for them to forget it. It might be something you felt was trivial, a throwaway remark, but which had an unforeseen impact on the recipient, perhaps hurting their feelings or making them feel differently about you. It is important to be aware of the risks you are taking when you speak without thinking about the impact your remarks may have on another person.

With regard to physical activities, you will find risks that may be considered very serious, as the outcome can have a huge impact on your life. If someone takes a walk along a footpath they should be quite safe. However, if they run and take a wrong step, they may sprain their ankle or even break a leg.

Certain sporting activities, such as playing rugby, horse riding or mountaineering, present serious risks, where the chance of getting injured is almost inevitable. Even seemingly safe activities, such as playing football or doing gymnastics can be dangerous. It is possible to reduce the risks by proper training, careful preparation and obeying the rules, and this should always be borne in mind when participating in such activities.

It is not possible to live life without taking any risks, indeed it would be a most boring and unadventurous life that had no risks in it at all, but in order to reduce to a minimum the possibility of a bad outcome, it is important to take necessary precautions and to assess thoroughly your mental and physical attitudes before embarking on a risky venture.

The Importance of Money

Although a happy life depends essentially on your intellect, your mind and above all, your attitude, the biggest problems and difficulties that you encounter in your daily life may be created by money.

It is not just the lack of money itself, which on its own creates pressures that can escalate into serious problems. Lack of money also creates tension between people. If you lend someone money, your relationship with that person immediately changes, though this may be a minor change from your point of view if you are confident that they will repay you. The borrower, on the other hand, may feel uncomfortable knowing that they now have an obligation to you, namely to pay you back. Such a small matter can cause a major change in the relationship between two people. Imagine the conflict if a borrower cannot or does not want to repay the loan and is constantly pressed for repayment by the lender. Eventually, even the closest friendship will suffer. Many people prefer to give the money to the other person as a gift instead of lending it, to avoid just such a situation developing and affecting their relationship adversely.

The availability and the correct management of money, be it small sums or larger amounts, is essential for a happy, smooth running life. If you manage your finances carefully, there should be no tight corners, no arguments. Keep your wishes within your reach and within your budget, and you should be able to fulfil them. This will help you to be more content and also allow you to assist others. The bottom line is always to keep your expectations and your expenditure within the limits of your income, and to stay away from any undertakings and commitments that you might not be able to meet.

It is clearly desirable to strive for an adequate income for the lifestyle you wish to have. This depends on your education, the trust others have in you, and most importantly on hard work. Assuming they are doing the same job, someone who works a 60 hour week will earn more than someone who works a 40 hour week.

It is also of vital importance to start saving at an early age. Money properly invested generates income, thereby adding to the money that you receive for your work. Initially, the accumulation of funds is only possible by saving. Even young children should be encouraged to start saving money on a regular basis, no matter how small the amount. It will grow over the years and when the child reaches 15 or 16 years old, it should have grown to such an extent that it will be earning a reasonable amount of interest. Once the child reaches maturity, they can invest it themselves, or perhaps use it towards their further education.

However, this is not the only reason for saving money. The availability of even a small fund gives you a certain freedom. If you have the urge to do something, or to buy something, you can fulfil your wish by using some of your savings. Above all, you will also enjoy a sense of security because, thanks to your savings, minor emergencies, whatever their nature, can be dealt with. Saving is thus a prerequisite for a feeling of security in life.

Most people develop a specific understanding of this monetary security as soon as they become aware of the importance of money. An 18 year old might have a good sense of security knowing they had saved 3,000 monetary units. Whereas the parents of a young family might need 30,000 monetary units in a savings account to feel secure. Extravagant expenses, such as the acquisition of a car or going on holiday, should be postponed until the need for security, at whatever level, is satisfied.

Try to remember the following rules:
- Thriftiness is essential to a secure and happy life
- Never borrow money or lend money to anybody
- Try not to incur any debts
- If you do have debts, pay them off at the earliest opportunity
- Always respect the value and importance of money in life

The Difficulty of Saying 'No'

All actions contain on the one hand an opportunity, and on the other hand, a risk. Sometimes this is referred to as the upside (the opportunity) and the downside (the risk involved). In everything we do, we strive to see that the upside is greater than the downside.

Occasionally we are put into a position where the downside, or risk, seems considerably greater than the upside, or opportunity. In this situation, we might prefer not to go with the opportunity or do what is expected of us. A firm 'No' is required.

It is generally more difficult to say 'No' than 'Yes'. This is because 'Yes' signifies approval, which is much more pleasant, particularly as far as the other person is concerned. 'No' signifies disapproval, meaning you oppose the other person's expectations or proposals.

This is why people often find it hard to say 'No', and there are people who appear to be unable to simply say 'No'. They are afraid to disappoint or disagree with others. Saying 'No' requires a certain degree of determination and toughness. However people who always follow the 'Yes' route, sometimes against their better judgement, will often land in difficult situations, compared with those who have the courage to say 'No'.

How can we make it easier for ourselves to say 'No'?

First of all, consider saying 'No' as part of a selling process. Try to persuade the other person that it might be better to abandon the original proposal or plan and do things differently, with a more positive attitude and, potentially, a better outcome.

If this appears to be too difficult, or even impossible, you could try to get out of the situation by finding an excuse, for example by saying that because of certain circumstances, the time is wrong for you to follow their suggestion.

As a last resort, you could offer a white lie, for example pretending to have a headache in an attempt to get out of a situation and to avoid giving a direct 'No' that might offend.

Remember, saying 'No' is often a sign of strength and sometimes can be the wisest decision.

To Be Tough

Many people do not have good self-control. They react instantly when faced with something that might cause them slight inconvenience or minor suffering. As soon as they feel overwarm, they remove some clothing and go round opening windows. As soon as it gets cooler, they put on extra clothing or turn on the heating. When they experience a slight pain, they believe they must be seriously ill and take medication, or even retire to bed.

This can be attributed to their state of mind, because they have never learned to exercise self-control and be tough with themselves. A certain mental discipline is essential in life, to make one less susceptible to the minor mishaps we all inevitably encounter. Those who are oversensitive will find their path through life much tougher, as they constantly over-react to small problems and inconveniences.

This mental sensitivity does not refer exclusively to physical discomfort. Many things in life are uncomfortable and can require mental toughness. Most people sometimes feel disinclined to do the activities they should be doing, such as studying, reading for educational purposes, practising sport or music and above all, working. This may be due to laziness, lethargy, lack of interest, or the presence of more interesting distractions, but it is also down to a lack of self-discipline. People with good self-discipline will ignore these feelings or distractions, and commit themselves fully to the task.

You need to develop a certain degree of mental toughness in order to become less susceptible to the distractions that may confront you. This toughness and self-discipline will help you to achieve your aims and to sail through life more easily and smoothly.

The Learning Curve

We are exposed to learning not only while we are in school and in formal education, but throughout our entire lives. Everyone's desire for knowledge differs, however the extent of our desire for information determines how much energy we direct towards the absorption and digestion of learning and wisdom.

Children are eager to get to know their environment and to learn about their relationship with their surroundings. That is a natural process. Later, getting to know the immediate environment is replaced by getting to know yourself, developing an understanding of your own potential and limitations. A large part of adult life is taken up by the need to earn a living and to find a way to live in harmony with your environment.

In our modern world, with its ever-changing environments, circumstances and situations, you are expected to adapt continuously and re-orientate yourself throughout your entire life. This is why nowadays people are judged primarily by what they have learnt in formal education and how successful they were in acquiring learning skills. If you have never learnt how to acquire knowledge fast and efficiently, you may not be able to cope with challenges at work and you could find it hard to get a job and earn a living.

We are all expected to be open to changes that take place and to readjust our old ideas and accept new ways of working. It is essential that you keep an open mind, develop a thirst for knowledge and cultivate an acceptance of change, as these are vital for success in today's fast-moving world.

In order to cope with life's continuous changes and demands, it is essential to come to terms with your own mental capabilities and the environment in which you live at a young age. Each of us must find and establish our own guide beam and focus on it to keep ourselves on track. It is all too easy to become distracted by other activities, which may be very interesting and appealing, but will take us off our course.

There is not enough time in our lives to explore thoroughly the vast sea of knowledge, full of interesting and enjoyable things, that is available to us all nowadays. You should therefore concentrate on relatively few things, in order to understand them fully. That way you will find fulfilment and satisfaction.

Rhythms

Our lives take place in the centre of wavelike events or rhythms to which we constantly have to adapt. We live with seasonal rhythms such as spring, summer, autumn and winter, all of which influence our physical and mental abilities. The moon and sun also emanate rhythms. Weather changes and variations in altitude or climate when we travel affect us in varying degrees. Our body must deal with these differences and adapt to these new rhythms. They affect us all, although they may affect people in different ways and to a greater or lesser extent.

Everybody follows his or her own biorhythms, which consist of rhythmic sequences affecting our entire metabolism and hence life itself. The more regular these sequences are, the more the mechanical and chemical processes taking place within our bodies will be enhanced.

For example, look at sleeping habits. 'Early Birds' are people who tend to be very active and creative in the morning and prefer to go to bed in the early evening. Others, sometimes referred to as 'Night Owls', work better and are more active in the evening. They prefer not to get up early in the day and often do not function well before noon.

The reason for this is based on our individual need for the period of deep sleep, which lasts for three to four hours of our total sleeping time. Early Birds need this deep sleep before midnight, while Night Owls prefer to get their deep sleep in the early hours of the morning.

We all have different prime times. In other words, we each have a period in the day when we function at our best. This may also vary according to what you are doing — you might be best at mental activities in the morning, but better at physical activities in the early evening.

The same applies to other processes that take place in our bodies, such as the digestive process. Each of us is affected differently, depending on what time we eat our meals, take our rest, and when we exercise.

The more you understand your own biorhythms, the more able you are to organise your life more efficiently and live your life in tune with your own particular rhythms. The more you live and work in conflict with your biorhythms, the greater the demands placed on your mind and body. It is therefore essential to live in harmony with your biorhythms and, as far as possible, in tune with the external rhythms in your environment that you cannot control.

Time flows like the current of a river through all mental, social and commercial activities. People who act intuitively or according to sensible considerations and swim with the flow have a much greater chance to be successful in life. People who try to swim against the tide will constantly experience difficulties and come up against problems, and consequently are likely to have a harder life.

To live in harmony with the flow of time depends on your sensibilities, your intuition and your understanding of the greater rhythms of life, and should ultimately lead you to a more satisfying and fulfilling life.

Judgment of Character

It is desirable, through knowledge and observation over the years, to acquire enough experience to be able to accurately assess the characters of other people. The degree of trust we are able to place in others, as well as our personal relationship with them, depends on this assessment. You need to be aware that during the process of assessment, both you and the other person are trying to show yourselves in the best possible light and to win each other's trust — it is a two-way operation.

The best way to assess others is by following the advice already given: write down 10 values which are important to you, and once you have formed an opinion of the other person, determine their own sequence of values. This should take relatively little time, perhaps only a few minutes, however with casual introductions, or in work meetings, you would have neither the time nor, possibly, the inclination to follow this method. In that situation, you have to make a quick mental assessment.

During our journey through life we continually make

judgments about others. Based on first impressions, it is possible to allocate most people to one of the following three groups. Over the course of time, as you get to know them better, you may decide they belong in a different group.

The open-hearted person

What you see is what you get. These people are exactly what they seem to be. They are transparent in the true sense of the word, candid, open and frank. You can easily perceive their way of thinking and see their emotions on their faces and in their body language. Their assessment is not difficult, you can usually trust them and they are easy to get on with.

The reserved person

It is more difficult to assess a reserved person. They do not show their true nature readily and it can take a long time before they reveal themselves or show their feelings. If they are in the right mood and feeling more relaxed, perhaps because of certain circumstances, such as under the influence of alcohol, you may gain some insight into their personality, but you cannot completely rely on it as they may be acting out of character. Reserved people require some effort to get on with, and forming a close relationship with them over a relatively short period of time is unlikely to happen. A deep relationship may become possible once you get to know them properly and trust is established.

The actor

The third group consists of people who are pretenders. They tend to play a role and intentionally try to deceive you or throw you off track. They possess certain mannerisms and often use humour as a mask to hide their true feelings or character. These people are very difficult to assess, especially as they have the ability to change their role according to how they want to be perceived. You cannot rely on them and should beware of deceptions and disappointments in relationships with such people.

The Definition of the Soul

If you believe that your soul matures during its many lives, you could also assume that the soul itself decides on the manner in which it wants to mature during its life on Earth and the experiences it wants to undergo. It is possible – and various religions preach this – that the soul even selects the parents who will bring it into the world in the form of a baby. This means that the genetics of the child to be born are already predetermined by the soul's choice of parents.

In addition, to gain maturity the soul wants to experience specific events and situations that have their origin in circumstances determined by humans. It could be that these experiences are gained through a life full of suffering and misfortune or, alternatively, through a life of happiness and well-being. It is more likely to be a blend of both. By controlling your mind and thoughts you can determine your environment to some extent, so you can influence the life experiences you, and your soul, gains.

Remember that life consists, on the one hand, of practising new skills that you need or want, and on the other hand, your search for new knowledge and new experiences.

Although a conflict could be created between the choice of parents and the soul's desire for a specific environment and experiences, such a conflict is unlikely, as the soul can make the choice of both. Genetic selection, that is, the choice of the parents, would be the way the soul ensured it would undergo experiences that would help it on its path to maturity — its ultimate aim.

The maturing process of the soul allows each of us to achieve a better understanding of life, in all the lives we live.

If you believe in the maturing process of the soul, which comprises experiencing a multitude of lives, you must conclude that all the souls, or people, you encounter during your life on Earth are similarly in a state of transition. This should lead to the realisation that you should not be too harsh, judgemental or didactic in your criticism of others. Just like your own soul, their souls are also in a state of development on the path to maturity.

Tolerance and empathy should be your touchstones, always, in your dealings with others.

Prudence

This section is to some extent a summary of what I have explained so far.

The structure of prudence can be illustrated in a different way, however for the purpose of simplifying, it is best summarised as follows:

Mental prudence means our direction through life is based on:

a) a long-term vision, including our hopes and dreams

b) a clear picture of what is to be achieved in the future, structured by setting short-term goals to be reached within a period of three years

c) a specific plan of action for the coming year

Physical prudence means:

a) taking care of your health in all its aspects

b) avoiding unnecessary risks, so being careful, deliberate and thoughtful

Prudent use of time requires:
  a) the understanding and proper utilisation of time,
     which means understanding your priorities,
     balancing all the different pressures made on you,
     and working with your internal rhythms and the
     rhythms of the natural world
  b) the desire not to waste time

Prudent use of our experiences and knowledge means we
should:
  a) try to absorb all the experiences and knowledge we
     are offered
  b) relax, and use the soft-selling method when learning
     and also when delivering information
  c) have a structure for all activities and interactions
     with others, with a clear plan, taking reason,
     emotion and intuition into consideration

If you try to follow the above guidelines, this will help to
keep you focused on a straight course, ultimately leading
you to a successful and fulfilling life.

Excessive Demands

It is possible to demand too much of yourself. For example, you can push yourself to work exceedingly hard in school, during further education and in your profession. You might participate in sports and pursue other interests such as music, theatre, reading, watching television and films, or spending time with friends and socialising as much as possible. Apart from the fact that, due to a lack of time, it may be impossible to do many of these activities well, such pressure and over-exertion may also mean that something that is crucial for your well-being has to suffer as a consequence.

Excessive demands can affect the standard of your work, and the quality of your friendships, and your ability to be successful in your various interests. However primarily it affects your health. We only have so much energy, and we cannot use more than we produce.

The Peter Principle is well known in professional circles. Under normal circumstances, everybody reaches a position in their profession that corresponds to their abilities. However if they are promoted to a higher post, it may become evident that this role demands more than they can offer. They will try their utmost to fulfil their colleagues, and the company's expectations, and they may even try to hide the fact that they are not capable of handling the tasks they are faced with. Very often, this will lead to the person putting excessive demands on themselves, to try to cope with the pressures of the job. Their health and their relationship with their family may suffer. Eventually the pressure may be such that they will be removed from the position, by being sacked or made redundant. Consequently, they may go from being so successful that they were promoted, to an absolute low in their professional life, perhaps even out of work.

It is therefore extremely important to recognise your limitations, and be aware of asking too much of yourself and of others — it may end in disaster.

On the other hand, neither should you demand too little of yourself. This would be equivalent to wasting your abilities and your time.

The goal is to find a balance between your energy and abilities, and between the demands made by others and by you. Spending a lot of time on amusements such as watching television, playing computer games, going out clubbing and partying can have a very negative, energy-draining effect, putting you under unnecessary pressure. However constructive recreational activities can be very beneficial, helping you to relax, and time should be found for these.

Excessive demands or pressures are sometimes referred to by a word often heard in our modern world, namely 'stress'. Moderate stress is normal and desirable. It mobilises the beneficial production of hormones such as adrenaline and readies us for action. However any change from a normal level of stress can have a negative impact on your physical functions, such as your blood pressure and your digestive process. We may not be aware of these fluctuations, and constant stress can lead to problems with some of these processes.

If you increase the level of stress you are feeling by putting yourself under pressure with excessive demands, stress can become a burden. This can manifest itself in various physical reactions that can lead to the deterioration of your well-being and affect your mental and spiritual state of mind, as well as your physical condition.

The Future of Luxury

It is very likely that in the future, luxury will no longer be measured by the possession of consumer goods such as expensive cars, designer clothing, jewellery or similar items. None of these things in themselves are necessary for a satisfying and fulfilling life.

On the contrary, in the future people will turn towards things that are precious because they are scarce but nevertheless essential for a fulfilling life, such as time and peace.

Time

Nowadays, excessive demands are made on us by a myriad of pressures, from family and friends, work, our personal interests and activities, and also our environmental circumstances. The result of all these pressures is that our time has become extremely precious.

In future, it will no longer be considered a luxury to jet across the ocean in a few hours in an aeroplane. On the contrary, it will be seen as a luxury to have the time to cross the ocean in four or five days on a liner. People can only live in luxury if they have the time to do what they want to do and if they themselves can decide how much time to spend on something, and where and when to do it.

Priorities

In today's chaotic world, with the internet, an abundance of TV channels, innumerable activities available, and advertising everywhere we look, it is virtually impossible to decide what should be given priority and what can be ignored. It will therefore be regarded as a luxury to be able concentrate just on those things that we really wish to see, hear, feel and know.

Space

Many of us live in an increasingly congested environment, not only in our towns and cities, but on our roads, in shops and restaurants, in stations and airports, and so on. We live surrounded by other people, in small flats or houses which are often filled to the maximum with furniture, appliances, electrical equipment and other paraphernalia, which can produce a feeling of claustrophobia, or even imprisonment.

What is missing is space. Space allows us to breathe, it encourages unencumbered movement and gives us the freedom to think. An almost empty room not only looks luxurious and larger, it also offers a sense of freedom. Buying fewer items and getting rid of clutter will enable you to live in a more luxurious and satisfying way.

Peace

It is becoming more and more difficult to live in quiet, peaceful surroundings. Many of us have to listen all day long to the noise of traffic, aeroplanes, televisions, radios and other sources of music or speech, as well as the sound of other people if we live or work in close proximity to them. Some people prefer always to have sound, usually music, in the background. However, for other people, being able to get away from this, to escape from the noise and find peace and quiet, perhaps even complete silence, is considered a great luxury.

The environment

In most cities, many large conurbations and virtually all industrialised areas, you can neither breathe clean air nor drink clean water. Many of the foods we eat are contaminated with toxic chemicals. It is therefore seen as utter luxury to spend your life breathing clean, fresh air, drinking pure water and eating uncontaminated fresh food that does not contain any toxins, preservatives or unnatural substances.

Security

Due to ever increasing numbers of underprivileged and dispossessed people from all over the world, a state can no longer guarantee the safety of its citizens. In most large cities there are areas where you cannot go after dark for fear of being attacked. Affluent citizens often live behind high walls and surround themselves with intensive security measures such as closed circuit cameras, to protect themselves.

In the future it is possible that the only people who will live in luxury will be those who can afford to live and work in an environment that offers a feeling of security. This could be achieved through protection and security measures, but how much better would it be if it was because the society in which they lived was fair to all, and so there was little risk of crime.

It is noticeable that a sizeable number of younger people in the developed world are not particularly interested in possessions, certainly less so than many of their parents and grandparents. Above all, they want to live a safe and comfortable life, with time to appreciate the simple things, space to feel free, peace and quiet when they want it, and a clean and secure environment.

Conclusion: Faith

Reflecting on these guidelines and in an attempt to find an all-embracing concept incorporating the various points of view and advice that I have offered, and which has the power to influence us and our environment, I have come to the conclusion that this overarching principle should be called Faith.

Let me explain. Firstly, everything you see or experience is seen or experienced through your own eyes and ears. We all believe what our senses tell us; for example that something is a certain colour or shape. At the same time, we know that other people have seen or encountered the same things as us, but they will have experienced it through different eyes, seen it in a different light as it were. It is your own personal vision, or faith, that allows you to understand and interpret yourself and your surroundings.

Secondly, faith has another significant connotation. Virtually all humans are in need of spiritual guidance. They want to believe in truth, the authenticity of values, and the reliability and integrity of those who make it their business to regulate their lives, or bring people together to work in harmony and reach common goals. Most people would also like to believe in a divine power and to understand the meaning of their life. How would you find your course, or guide beam, without being able to understand the meaning, or recognise the purpose, of all your efforts and activities throughout your life? Only through having faith in a higher purpose.

The need for faith is a fundamental need of all people.

The strength of faith is most impressive. In the Scriptures we read that faith can move mountains. The history of humankind tells us that people with a strong faith, who are completely focused on reaching a certain goal, have a particular aura that attracts others. We see this in religion and in politics, in the business world and in sport. Prominent people in history emanated this aura or charisma and often had many followers, primarily due to their radiation of an unusually strong faith. Their personalities and activities sometimes brought them peaceful, happy lives, and sometimes led them and their followers to perdition and ruin.

It is important to remember that your faith can have a strong influence on your life and on your environment. Faith not only determines your direction in life but also helps you to focus your energies, giving you the strength needed to follow your path through life.

If you believe very strongly in something, you will behave in such a way that should enable you to attain what you believe in.

Faith and knowledge should be balanced, creating a harmony within your life and within your environment, enabling you to live your life in such a way that it is fulfilling, satisfying and ultimately, happy.

Acknowledgements

During my life, books by the two people below have provided me with inspiration and guidance, helping me to formulate my own ideas and thoughts about moral, philosophical and spiritual issues.

Khalil Gibran – 1883-1931

Gibran was born in Lebanon, and as a young man emigrated with his family to the United States. He was an artist, poet and writer, chiefly known in the English-speaking world for his 1923 book *The Prophet*, an example of inspirational writing that includes a series of philosophical essays. One of the bestselling books of the twentieth century in the US, *The Prophet* has been continuously in print since it was first published and has been translated into over forty languages.

Emmet Fox – 1886-1951

Born in Ireland, Fox moved to the United States in his late 20s, where he became a spiritual leader in the New Thought movement. A scientist, philosopher and spiritual teacher, he would address huge gatherings of people, expressing his thoughts on the religious meaning of life. He published seven books, the best known of which are *The Sermon on the Mount*, and *Power through Constructive Thinking*. After his death a collection of his work was published with the title *Around the Year With Emmet Fox: A Book of Daily Readings*.